THIS COLORING BOOK
BELONGS TO

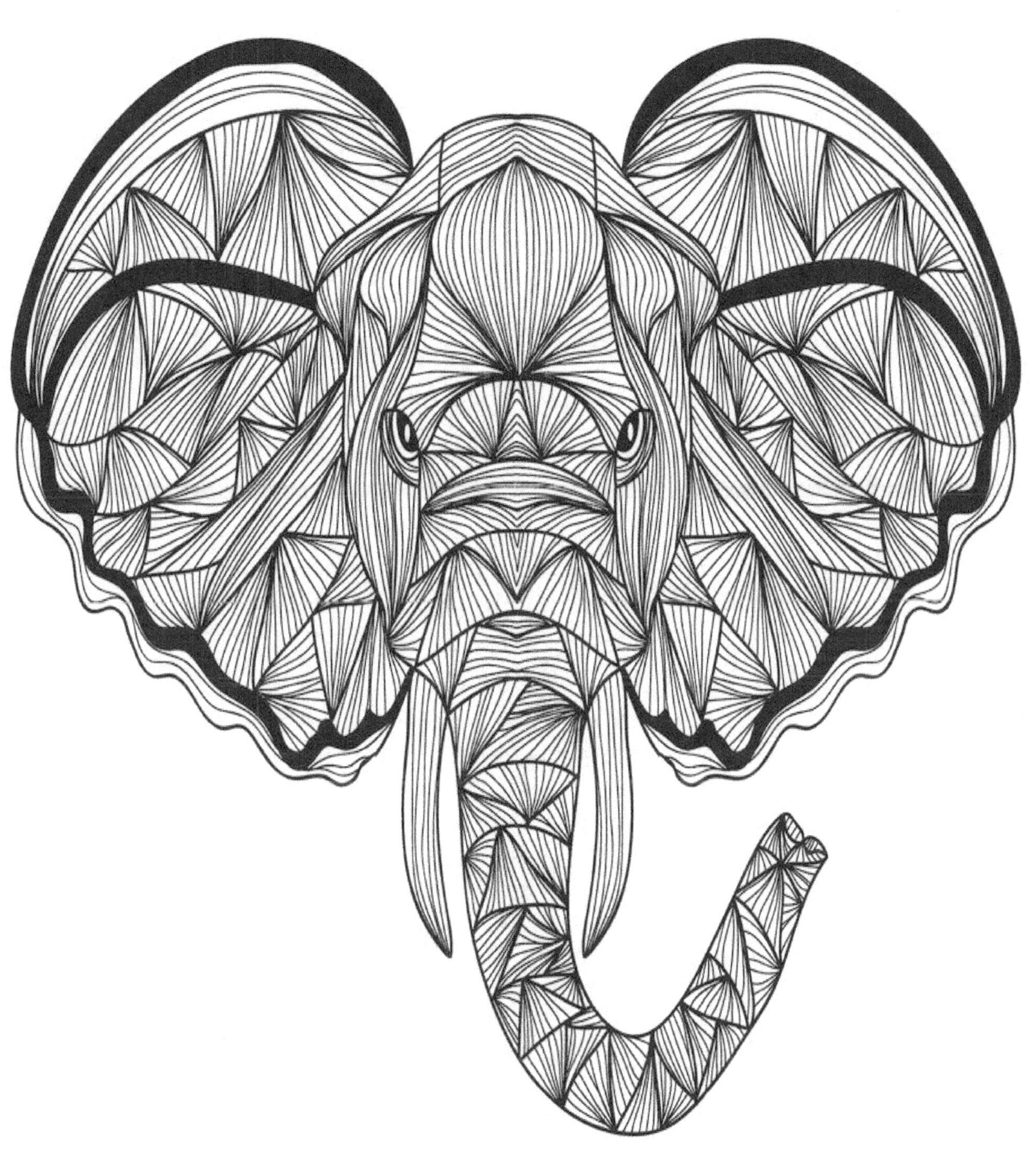

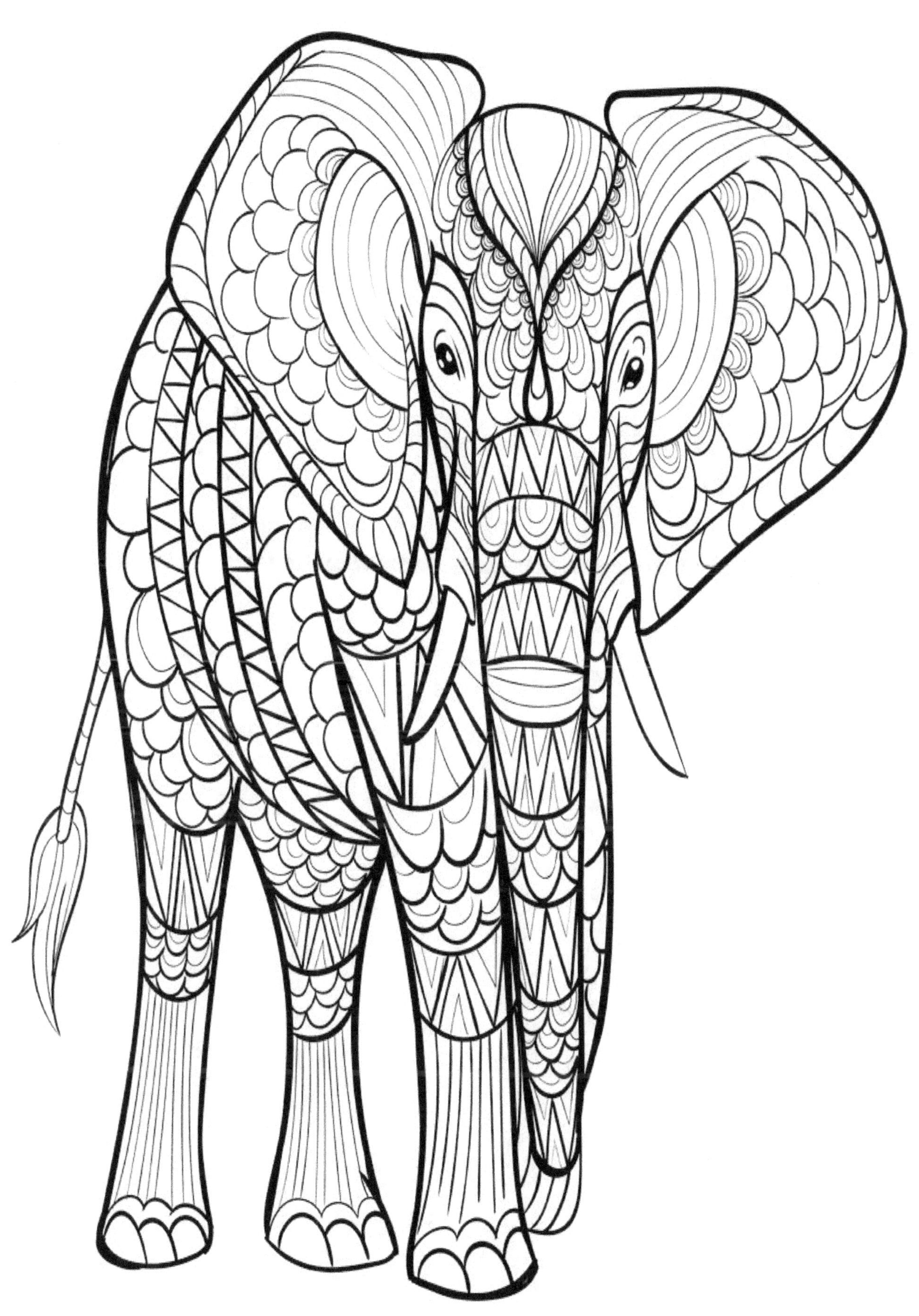

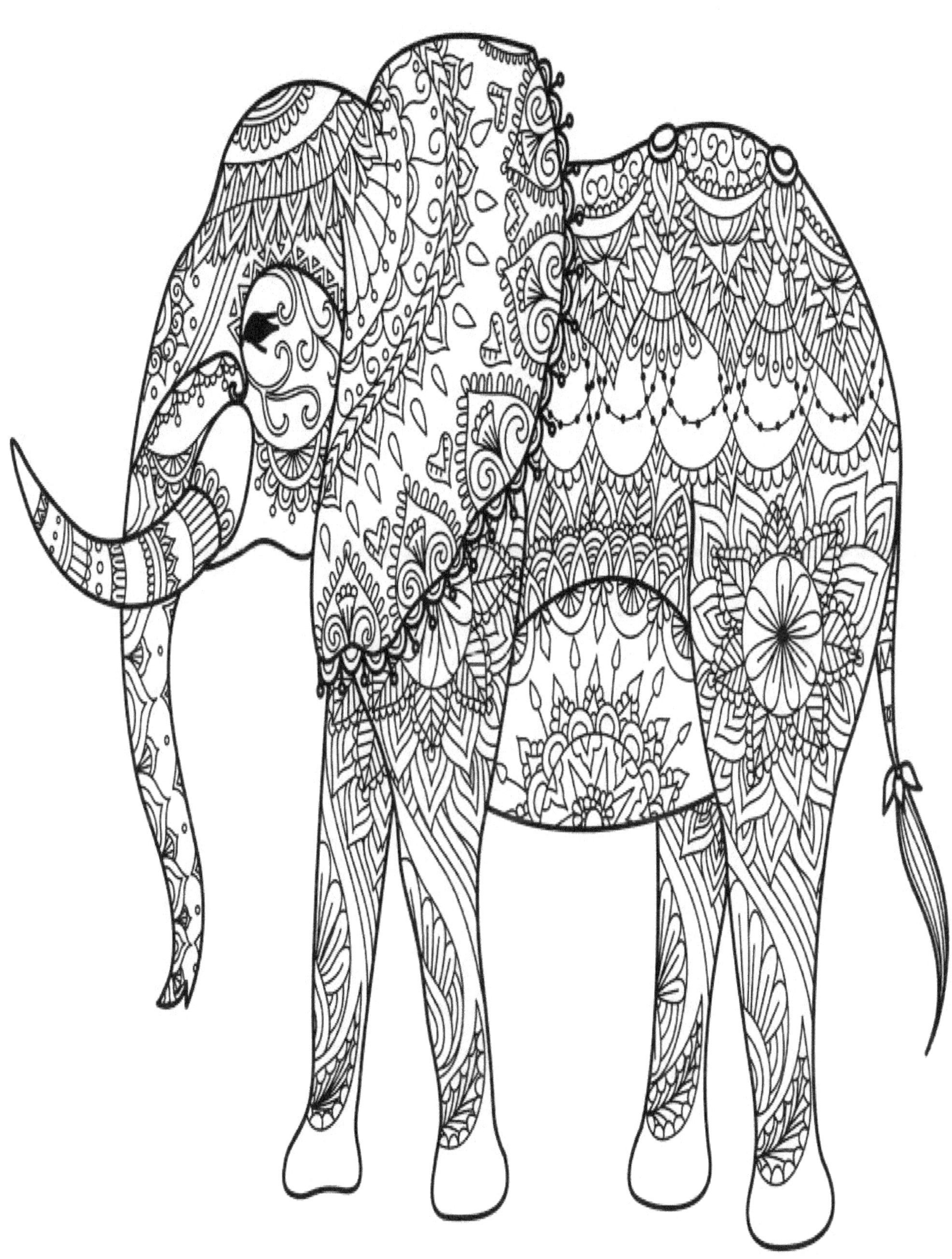

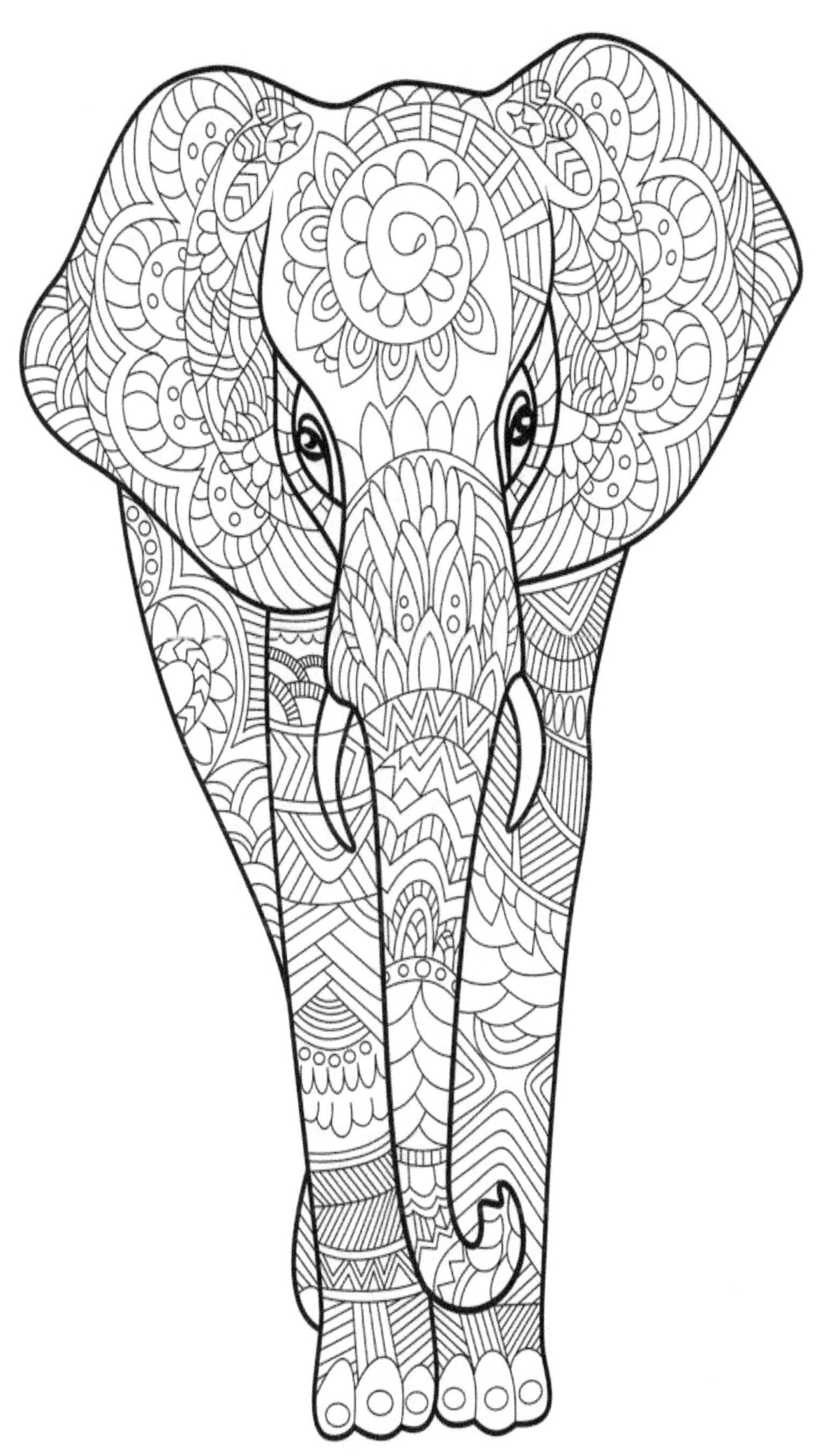

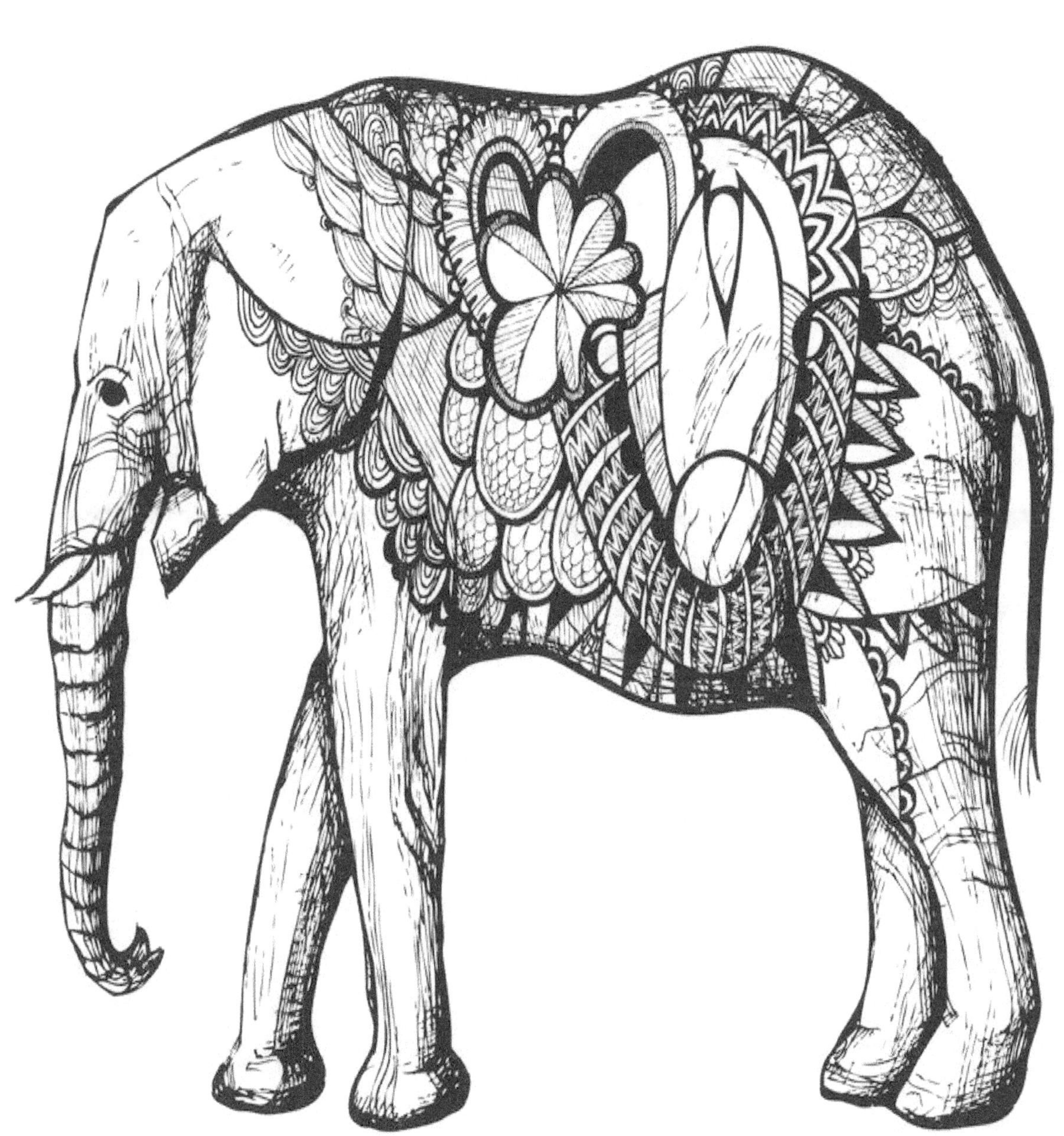

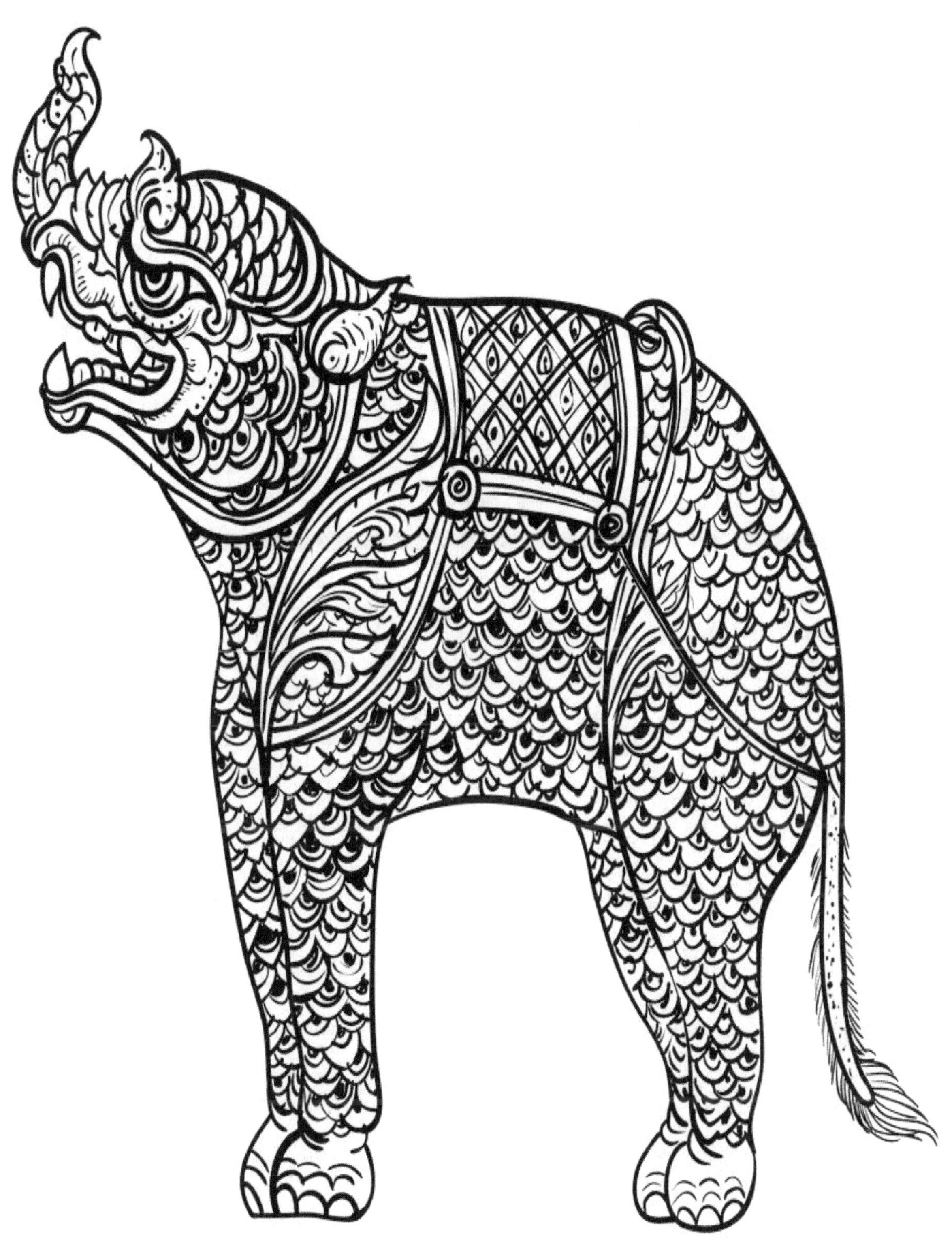

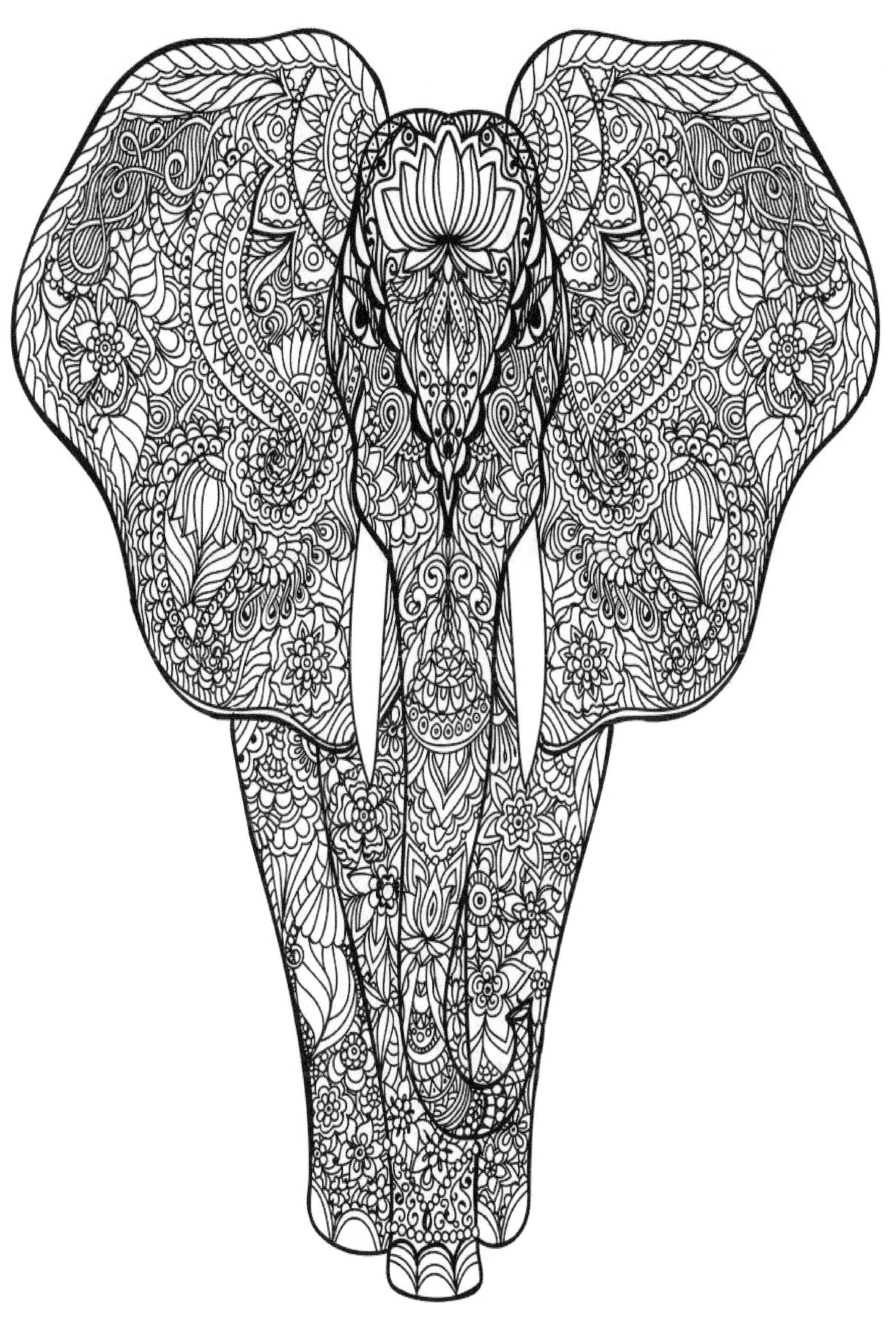